HEROES OF BLACK HISTORY

JACKIE ROBINSON

BY KATIE KAWA

Gareth Stevens PUBLISHING

Please visit our website, www.garethstevens.com. For a free color catalog of all our high-quality books, call toll free 1-800-542-2595 or fax 1-877-542-2596.

Library of Congress Cataloging-in-Publication Data

Names: Kawa, Katie, author.
Title: Jackie Robinson / Katie Kawa.
Description: New York : Gareth Stevens Publishing, [2019] | Series: Heroes of black history | Includes index.
Identifiers: LCCN 2018015525| ISBN 9781538230183 (Library bound) | ISBN 9781538231302 (Paperback) | ISBN 9781538233108 (6 pack)
Subjects: LCSH: Robinson, Jackie, 1919-1972–Juvenile literature. | African American baseball players–Biography–Juvenile literature. | Baseball players–United States–Biography–Juvenile literature.
Classification: LCC GV865.R6 K39 2019 | DDC 796.357092 [B] –dc23
LC record available at https://lccn.loc.gov/2018015525

First Edition

Published in 2019 by
Gareth Stevens Publishing
111 East 14th Street, Suite 349
New York, NY 10003

Designer: Katelyn E. Reynolds
Editor: Joshua Turner

Photo credits: Cover, pp. 1 (Jackie Robinson), 7, 8, 23, 27 Bettmann/Getty Images; cover, pp. 1–32 (background image), 14 courtesy of the Library of Congress; p. 5 Keystone/Getty Images; p. 6 Hulton Archive/Getty Images; p. 9 Sporting News/Sporting News via Getty Images; p. 13 Curt Gunther/Keystone/Archive Photos/Getty Images; p. 15 Transcendental Graphics/Getty Images; p. 17 J. R. Eyerman/The LIFE Picture Collection/Getty Images; p. 19 Nina Leen/Time & Life Pictures/Getty Images; p. 20 NY Daily News Archive via Getty Images; p. 21 Irving Haberman/IH Images/Getty Images; p. 25 Olen Collection/Diamond Images/Getty Images; p. 28 Rob Leiter/MLB Photos/Getty Images; p. 29 Focus On Sport/Getty Images.

Printed in the United States of America

CPSIA compliance information: Batch #CW19GS: For further information contact Gareth Stevens, New York, New York at 1-800-542-2595.

CONTENTS

Words in the glossary appear in **bold** type the first time they are used in the text.

BREAKING BARRIERS IN BASEBALL

Today, Major League Baseball (MLB) players come from many different countries, speak many different languages, and consist of many different races. That wasn't always the case, though. For a long time, professional baseball in the United States was segregated, or separated, by race. Only white baseball players could play for the American League (AL) or National League (NL).

That changed in 1947, when Jackie Robison became the first African American to cross baseball's color line, which kept black and white baseball players in separate leagues. By bravely breaking that **barrier**, Robinson became a hero both on and off the field.

AMERICA'S PASTIME

Baseball is often called "America's national **pastime**." The sport was created in the United States, although its exact inventor has been debated for many years. Baseball is still a very popular sport in the United States, and it has also spread around the world, especially in Asia and in Latin America.

Jackie Robinson was a great baseball player who helped fight for equal rights before, during, and after playing **professional** baseball for the Brooklyn Dodgers.

FROM GEORGIA TO CALIFORNIA

Jack Roosevelt Robinson was born on January 31, 1919, in Cairo, Georgia. He was the youngest of five children, and his family grew up without a lot of money. His mother, Mallie, raised her children on her own. They lived in the South at a time when African Americans were treated poorly and didn't have the same rights as white Americans.

Jackie and his family moved to Pasadena, California, when he was young. Athletics were a big part of Jackie's life while he was growing up. He played many different sports, including baseball, tennis, and basketball.

MACK ROBINSON

Jackie wasn't the only great **athlete** in his family. His older brother Matthew, who was also known as Mack, was a star in track and field. During the 1936 Olympics in Berlin, Germany, Mack Robinson won a silver **medal** for coming in second in the 200-meter dash.

Jackie Robinson, second from left, with his family

Jackie Robinson grew up in a time when African Americans didn't have the same opportunities as white Americans. Sports gave Jackie a way to be successful.

A DIFFERENT KIND OF FIGHT

Jackie Robinson went to college, but he never finished school. He joined the US Army in 1942. His time in the army taught him to stand up for his beliefs, even when it was hard.

In 1944, Robinson was told to sit in the back of a military bus because of the color of his skin. When he said he wouldn't do it, he was court-marshaled, which means he was put in front of a military court. The charges were eventually dropped, but Robinson continued to fight for civil rights for the rest of his life.

SCHOOL DAYS

Robinson went to college at the University of California, Los Angeles (UCLA), but left during his last year. At UCLA, he was a successful athlete in football, basketball, track and field, and baseball. After he left school, he continued to play sports. He even played football for a team in Hawaii called the Honolulu Bears.

Jackie Robinson at UCLA

Jackie Robinson served his country in the US Army during World War II, but he never fought in the war. He faced a different kind of battle instead—a fight to be treated fairly no matter the color of his skin.

PROFESSIONAL BASEBALL BEGINNINGS

After leaving the US Army, Robinson returned to the world of sports. He began his professional baseball career in 1945. At this time, white and black baseball players had to play in different leagues, so Robinson played in the all-black league known as the Negro American League.

Robinson played only one season in this league. He played shortstop for the Kansas City Monarchs. Shortstop is the position between second and third base on the baseball field. A shortstop has to be very skilled to be successful, and Robison showcased his skill throughout the 1945 season.

NEGRO LEAGUE BASEBALL

From the late 1800s to 1947, baseball was segregated. Black baseball players during this time played in what was known as the Negro leagues. Many famous baseball players from the Negro leagues crossed the color line after Jackie Robinson and became successful alongside their white teammates. These players included Satchel Paige, Hank Aaron, and Willie Mays.

BASEBALL POSITIONS

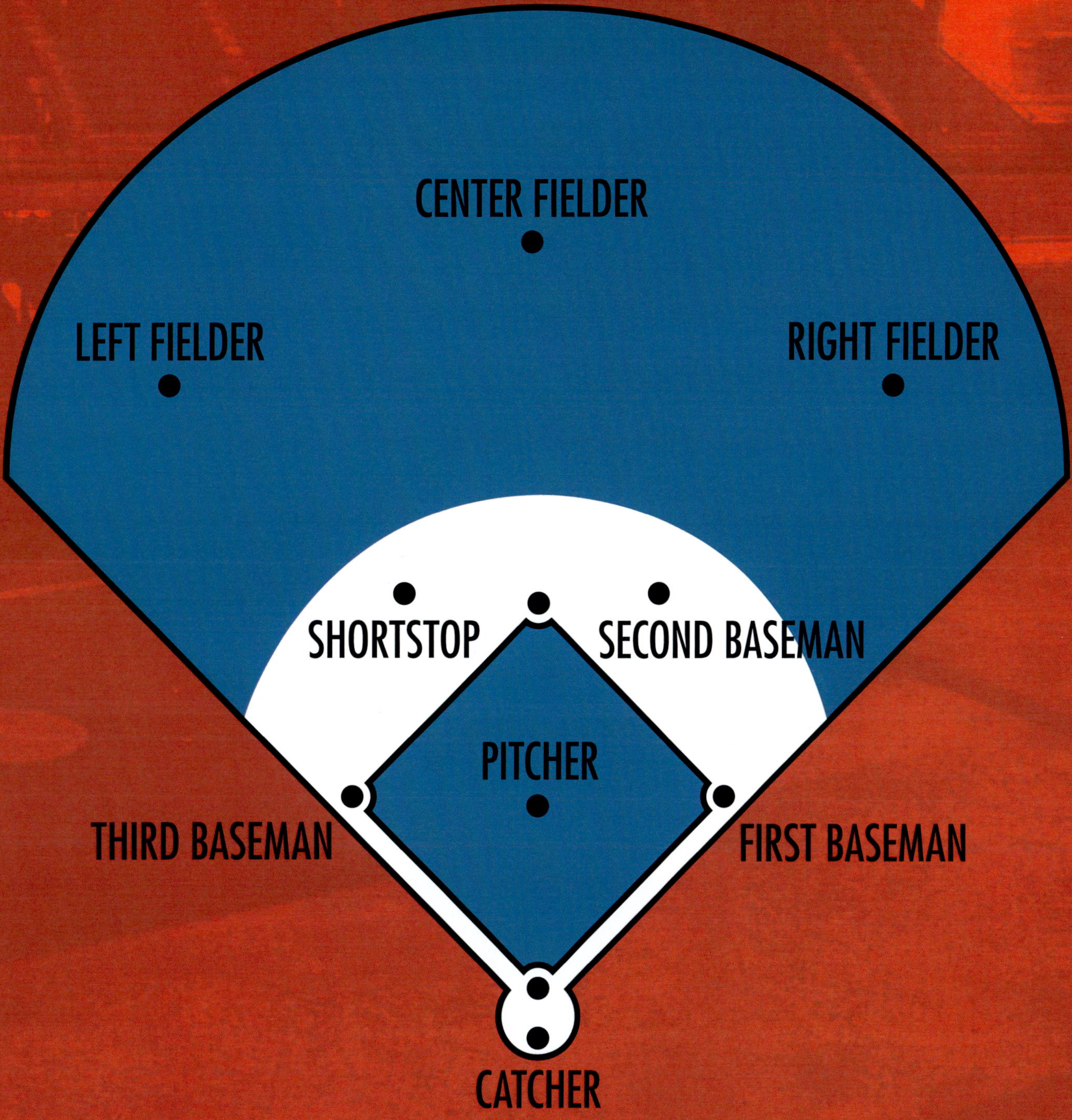

Jackie Robinson played many different positions on the baseball field, or diamond, throughout his career. He started as a shortstop for the Kansas City Monarchs, but he also played at first base, at second base, at third base, and in the outfield for the Brooklyn Dodgers.

ROBINSON AND RICKEY

Robinson's talent made him stand out on the field, and his character made him stand out off of it. He soon caught the eye of Branch Rickey, who was the president and general manager of the Brooklyn Dodgers at the time.

Rickey wanted to make baseball an integrated sport, which means black and white athletes would play on teams together. He needed to find the right man to be the first to cross the color line, and he believed Robinson was that man. He saw Robinson's skill, calm **personality**, and family-friendly lifestyle as a winning combination that would make white fans accept him as a part of their team.

BRANCH RICKEY

Branch Rickey was a man with big ideas, and those ideas changed baseball forever. He created the farm system, which is the way players are trained for the major leagues by playing on minor league teams first. He also played a big part in the use of batting cages and helmets, in addition to his most famous idea: integrating baseball.

Branch Rickey (left) and Jackie Robinson helped each other make history!

"GUTS ENOUGH NOT TO FIGHT BACK"

Rickey and Robinson both knew that the road ahead would not be easy. Robinson was going to face many people who wanted him to go back to the Negro leagues, and Rickey wanted to make sure that Robinson could handle what those people would say and do to him.

Rickey tested Robinson's ability to stay calm as he was called names. Rickey even asked what Robinson would do if a white player tried to use the spikes on his shoes to hurt him. Rickey told Robinson he wanted a player "with guts enough not to fight back." This was hard for Robinson, but he knew he could do it.

THE SEGREGATED SOUTH

Jackie Robinson broke baseball's color barrier at a time when most other parts of life in the United States, especially in the South, were segregated. Laws created after the American Civil War, known as Jim Crow laws, took away many rights from African Americans and forced them to use separate schools, bathrooms, and even drinking fountains.

Jim Crow in America

Branch Rickey made Jackie Robinson promise that he wouldn't fight back—no matter how poorly he was treated. Many other civil rights heroes did the same. They had the strength to take the high road even when the people around them were unkind and hurtful.

MAKING IT OFFICIAL

Robinson impressed Rickey, and Rickey knew he'd found the best man to cross baseball's color line. In October 1945, Robinson signed a contract with the Brooklyn Dodgers. Before he could join the Dodgers on the field, though, he had to spend some time playing in the minor leagues, which most players do before joining their MLB team.

In 1946, Robinson began playing for the Montreal Royals in Canada, which was part of a minor league known as the International League. Robinson was a star for the Royals, leading the entire league in **batting average** and helping his team win a **championship**.

STOLEN BASES

Jackie Robinson was known throughout his career for his talent at stealing bases. A baseball player steals a base when he makes it safely from one base to the next without the ball being put into play. This often happens right before the pitcher throws the ball. During his season in Montreal, Robinson stole 40 bases!

Jackie Robinson was treated better in Montreal than he was in many parts of the United States.

A FAMILY MAN

Baseball wasn't the only thing on Robinson's mind at this time in his life. Family had always been important to him, and the image of him as a family man was one of the reasons he was chosen to break baseball's racial barriers.

In 1946, Jackie Robinson married Rachel Isum, whom he had met while at UCLA. She had been a nursing student. Eventually, she became the mother to the couple's three children: Jackie Jr., Sharon, and David. During Jackie's time with the Dodgers, his family had to deal with **threats** to their safety, but Rachel remained supportive of her husband's groundbreaking career.

THE LIFE OF RACHEL ROBINSON

Rachel Robinson was more than just the supportive wife of a baseball player. She was also a nurse who later became the nursing director for the Connecticut Mental Health Center. She also created the Jackie Robinson Foundation in 1973 to honor her husband by providing money for young people to get an education and leadership training.

Jackie and Rachel Robinson both became active in the civil rights movement.

A GROUNDBREAKING GAME

With his family by his side, Jackie Robinson made the leap to the big leagues on April 15, 1947, when he officially joined the Brooklyn Dodgers. On that day, he became the first African American to play in a Major League Baseball game in the 20th century. By stepping on the field in Brooklyn that day, he stepped into the history books.

Robinson had a very successful first year in Brooklyn. He stole 29 bases in 1947, which led the National League, and he hit 12 home runs. He was even named the National League Rookie of the Year, which is a title that is given to the best new player in the league.

A COACH IN HIS CORNER

Robison always had the support of his Dodgers coach (also known as a manager in baseball), Leo Durocher. When some Dodgers players spoke out against Rickey's decision to sign Robinson, Durocher had his new player's back. He told Robinson's white teammates that it didn't matter what color a player's skin was. All that mattered was how badly he wanted to win.

Jackie with coach Leo Durocher

Robinson is shown here with his teammates during his groundbreaking first game with the Dodgers at Ebbets Field in Brooklyn, New York.

CHANGE ISN'T EASY

Robinson's Rookie of the Year title showed that many people in baseball felt that he had earned his place in history. However, not everyone agreed. Robinson faced angry crowds of people who threw things at him and yelled awful insults about him and his family. He also had to stay in different hotels and eat in different restaurants while traveling with his white teammates in the segregated South.

Even other players treated Robinson poorly. They would try to hurt him as they slid into bases. Some of them even said they wouldn't play against the Dodgers, because they didn't want to share the field with a black man.

TEAMMATES AND FRIENDS

One famous story about Jackie Robinson is that when a crowd of fans was being tough on him during a game, the Dodgers shortstop, Pee Wee Reese, walked over to Robinson and put his arm around him. This sign of friendship and support supposedly quieted the crowd. Although no one is sure whether that actually happened, Reese and Robinson really did become lifelong friends.

Jackie Robinson was often treated poorly by fans and even other players, but he tried not to show anyone that it bothered him. He knew young people looked up to him, and he wanted to set a good example.

A TRUE MVP

Robinson once said, "I knew I was kind of an experiment. The whole thing was bigger than me." He knew he had to be a successful athlete and a good person to make the experiment work, and he generally let his play do the talking during his career.

Robinson played for the Dodgers for 10 seasons, and he led the team to six National League championships and its first World Series championship. In 1949, he led the league in stolen bases and batting average, which helped earn him the title of the National League's Most Valuable Player (MVP).

A HEROIC HALL OF FAMER

Robinson's success on the field and his place in sports history earned him a spot in the National Baseball Hall of Fame in 1962. He was the first African American to be honored in this way. Visitors to the National Baseball Hall of Fame and Museum in Cooperstown, New York, can learn much more about Robinson and other baseball heroes.

A CAREER IN NUMBERS

WORLD SERIES CHAMPIONSHIPS **1**

NATIONAL LEAGUE CHAMPIONSHIPS **6**

BATTING AVERAGE **.311**

AT BATS **4,877**

STOLEN BASES **197**

HOME RUNS **137**

Robinson changed baseball in a way that can't be measured by numbers. However, the numbers shown here add up to a very successful career.

LIFE AFTER BASEBALL

Robinson retired from baseball in 1957, but his work toward equality and civil rights for all people was just beginning. He supported and opened businesses with the goal of helping African American workers and communities. He also worked with church groups and young people.

Robinson became a more outspoken civil rights **activist** after his baseball career was done. He worked with the National Association for the Advancement of Colored People (NAACP) and became close friends with the famous civil rights leader Martin Luther King Jr.

A STORY WORTH TELLING

Jackie Robinson's story has been told in many books and movies. Robinson told his side of the story in the book *I Never Had It Made*, and his wife, Rachel, wrote the book *Jackie Robinson: An Intimate Portrait* in 1996. On the big screen, Robinson starred in the 1950 film *The Jackie Robinson Story*, and one of the latest movies about Robinson was *42*, which was released in 2013 and starred Chadwick Boseman as Robinson.

Robinson and King respected each other. When King went to jail for fighting for equal rights, Robinson held a concert to raise money to get him out.

AN IMPORTANT LIFE

Jackie Robinson's **legacy** has lived on long after his death on October 24, 1972. It survives in kids of all races dreaming of playing the sports they love. Robinson also made it easier for people to imagine a world in which black and white Americans worked together. That made it easier for civil rights leaders to fight for equal employment opportunities.

Robinson once said, "A life is not important except in the **impact** it has on other lives." He left a lasting impact and will always be known as an important part of sports history, black history, and American history.

JACKIE ROBINSON DAY

Exactly 50 years after Robinson broke the color barrier in baseball, it was announced that his **jersey** number, 42, would be retired by all MLB teams. This meant that no one else would ever wear it. However, on April 15 of each year—Jackie Robinson Day—players, coaches, and umpires all wear 42 to honor Robinson's impact on their sport.

Jackie Robinson Day, 2017

Jackie Robinson is still considered a hero to many African American athletes. He helped shaped not only the future of America's pastime but also the future of America as a nation.

GLOSSARY

activist: a person who uses or supports strong actions to help make changes in politics or society

athlete: someone who is physically fit and takes part in sporting events

barrier: something that makes progress hard

batting average: the number of hits a batter has, divided by his opportunities at bat

championship: a contest to find out who's the best player or team in a sport

impact: strong effect

jersey: a shirt worn by members of a sports team as part of a uniform

legacy: something that is passed down from someone

medal: a prize given to the winners of a competition. They are often made out of metal and worn on a ribbon around the neck.

pastime: an activity that is done often for enjoyment

personality: the set of qualities and ways of behaving that make a person different from other people

professional: earning money from an activity that many people do for fun

threat: a statement indicating that someone will be harmed if he or she does not do what someone else wants him or her to do

FOR MORE INFORMATION

BOOKS

Hetrick, Hans. *Breaking Barriers.* North Mankato, MN: Capstone, 2017.

Rice, Donna. *Jackie Robinson: Hometown Hero.* Huntington Beach, CA: Teacher Created Materials, 2017.

Strand, Jennifer. *Jackie Robinson.* Minneapolis, MN: ABDO Zoom, 2017.

WEBSITES

Baseball Hall of Fame
baseballhall.org
The official website of the National Baseball Hall of Fame and Museum has fun facts about Jackie Robinson and many other famous baseball players.

The Jackie Robinson Foundation
www.jackierobinson.org
This website features the work done by the Jackie Robinson Foundation, including ways to get involved in keeping Robinson's legacy alive.

PBS: Jackie Robinson
www.pbs.org/kenburns/jackie-robinson/
PBS takes visitors inside Jackie Robinson's life with a timeline, statistics, and videos.

Publisher's note to educators and parents: Our editors have carefully reviewed these websites to ensure that they are suitable for students. Many websites change frequently, however, and we cannot guarantee that a site's future contents will continue to meet our high standards of quality and educational value. Be advised that students should be closely supervised whenever they access the internet.

INDEX